People's Jobs

Paul Humphrey

Illustrated by

Beverley Lees

Evans

This is our town.

Let's go and meet some of them.
Lots of people work here.

This is the post office.
We buy stamps and send letters and parcels from here.

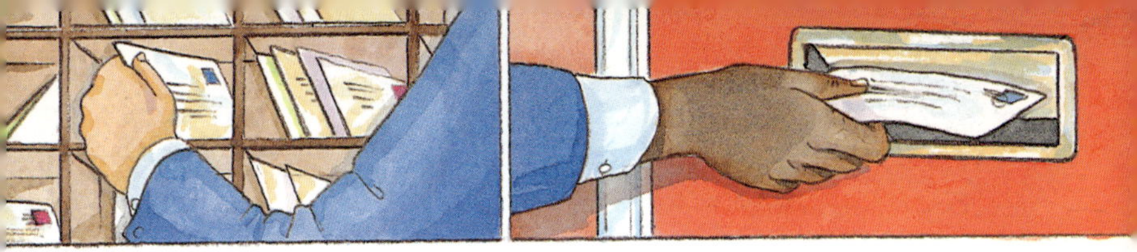

Behind the post office is the sorting office, where people sort the letters and parcels. Other postal workers deliver the mail across the country and overseas.

Here is our school.
Our teachers work here.

At the school the head teacher is in charge. There are cleaners, dinner staff, a caretaker and gardeners working here, too.

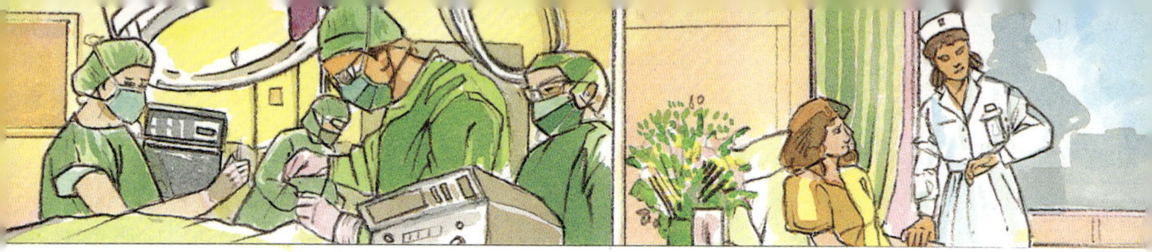

The doctors at the hospital made Mum better when she was ill.
I would like to be a doctor.

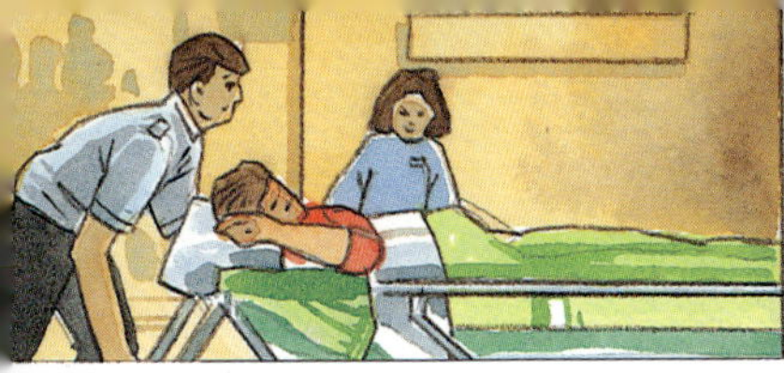

Hundreds of people work in a hospital. There are doctors, nurses, porters, ambulance drivers and chemists.

Then there are the people who work the x-ray machines, clerks, kitchen workers and cleaners.

Mum and Dad bring the car to be fixed at the garage.
The mechanic is checking the brakes.

Some garages sell cars and some garages have mechanics to repair cars.

At this garage mechanics make sure the cars and lorries are safe to drive. They change tyres, repair dents and check engines.

At the airport there are people checking the tickets...
...and there are people handling the baggage.

An airport is a busy, bustling place. There are also lots of people that you cannot see.

There are the pilots who fly the planes, engineers who make sure the planes are safe and hundreds more.

Some of the police officers in the police station wear uniforms...
...and some wear ordinary clothes.

The officers in ordinary clothes are detectives. They help to solve crimes. Police photographers and police scientists also work at the police station.

The hotel receptionist checks people into their rooms.
The porter carries guests' bags to their rooms.

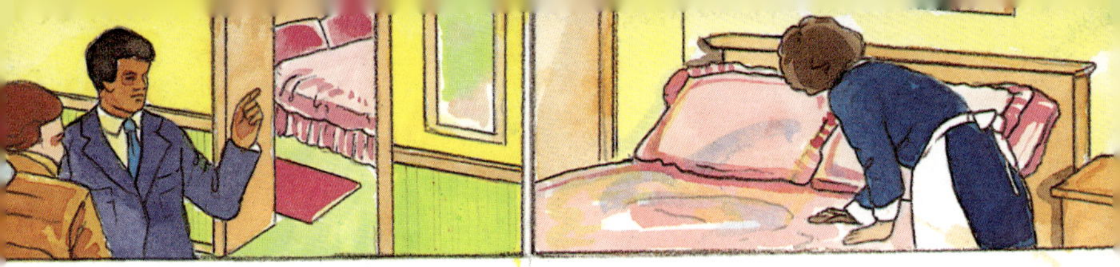

The hotel manager makes sure that everything runs smoothly. The chamber staff clean rooms and make beds.

There are chefs, waiters and waitresses in the hotel restaurant, too.

The newspaper office is a very busy place.
There are lots of computers here.

Journalists and reporters work for the newspaper editor. Then there are the people who help print the paper and those that deliver it to our doorsteps every day.

Everyone on the building site works very hard.
There's a builder laying bricks...

People have to work on building sites in all weathers. They have to work machines like bulldozers, dumper trucks, cranes and cement mixers.

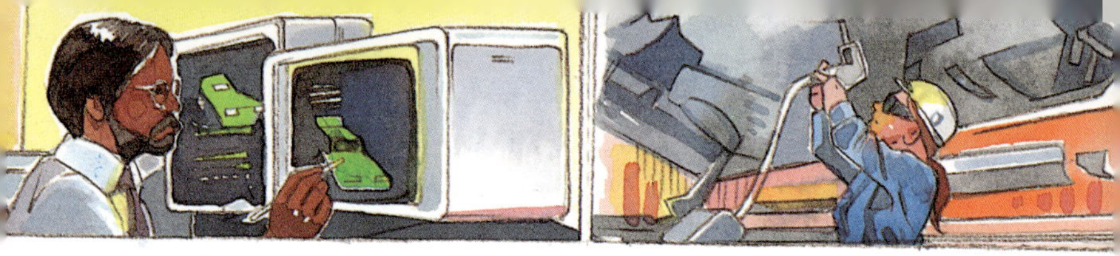

This is a huge factory!
All the people here are making cars.

In a car factory there are people who design and test cars. Then there are all the people who look after the machines, too.

We do our shopping here.

In a big supermarket there are the checkout staff, shelf fillers and the people who work in the warehouse.

Our last visit is to the town hall.
The people here run the whole town.

In the town hall people collect taxes and decide where all the money will be spent.

If you enjoyed the trip around the town, see if you can guess where each of these people works. The answers are at the bottom of the page, but don't peep until you have tried yourself.

1

2

3

4

1 garage 2 hotel 3 supermarket 4 hospital